the

chaos

of longing

The Chaos of Longing
©2016 by K. Y. Robinson
www.kyrobinson.net

First edition
ISBN-13: 978-0692649091
ISBN-10: 0692649093

to those who
lie awake
burning.

contents

epiphany

inception

blood

i'm half jerk chicken
and collard greens
suffocating
in this nightmare
called the american dream.

1.7.93

(i.)

i was an insecure
cocoa brown
hunchback girl
who swallowed poems
and never thought of
heaven or hell
when i met him.

i was thirteen
cursed with acne
and overripe breasts
longing to feel pretty.

he was twice my age,
a smooth talker,
and towered over me
like sugarcane.

in time
i learned
he wasn't so sweet.

(ii.)

before he undressed
he popped in a vhs
and insisted that we
reenact pornographic scenes.

i said no in sequences.
he told me to relax
as he disheveled
my innocence.

i was so paralyzed by fear
that my eyes refused
to summon tears.

i stared at the ceiling,
dispossessed every feeling,
and waited on god
to arrive and deprive
me of this unholy war.

god never came
but
he
did.

(iii.)

when it was over,
i feigned sleep
to keep him at bay
as he slept on a couch
just a few feet away.

my crouch housed
his milky filth
and my excrements.
it made a stew

that stench
of the death
of innocence.

i still remember
that smell
twenty-three
years later.

deferred

(i.)

i can't pinpoint
the moment
my father realized
america wasn't
what he thought
it would be.
he quelled
his rage with beer
and took up residence
on the bathroom floor.
i held my urine
and my disappointment
to keep myself from
drowning.

(ii.)

i can't pinpoint
the moment
when my mother
couldn't bring herself
to utter or accept
"i love you".
so i carved out
my own version of love
into the flesh of men—
to feel their heat rising
kept me
from unearthing

my predisposition
for shrinking.

(iii.)

i can't pinpoint
the moment
we all decided to stay
in the sun too long
to make raisins
of ourselves.
sucking the juice
out of ourselves
and withering
on the vine
of life.

faada

he only said
he loved me
when i was being
reprimanded.
that's when i learned
i had to tempt chaos
to feel loved.

mother's nature

i used to
turn away
from her
but now
i'm turning
into her
slowly
like honey.

faithless

you are the elephant
in the room that
i won't acknowledge
and too afraid to poach.

there are times
i want to press
my hands against
each other like lovers
and evict all doubts
but i always end up
with more questions
than answers.

magic

she has an air
about her
that suffocates
women like me
who are the epitome
of insecurity.

she stores magic
in her cheeks
and runs up a tree
when i ask for a piece.

i guess it's up to me
to find my own.
maybe i'll find some
on the way home.

manic depression

one moment life
is more pigmented
than technicolor.
glitter flows
through my veins
and the stars
in my eyes dilate
and burst
into delusions.

minutes, hours,
or days later
shades of blue and black
surround me like smoke.
glitter morphs
into chards of glass
and taunts every
breath i take.

stigma & shame

i carry all my hurt
like satchels.
i can only unpack
them on pages.

despair climbed
out of my throat
when i wasn't looking
and fell in my lap.

i wanted to jump
from my bones
and disperse
in the wind
like dandelion
seed heads—
to be free
and light as air.

i wanted to feel
the hot air of
anticipating mouths
bidding me farewell
as the wind carried me
into the next life
because i was suffocating
in the present one.

now i'm alone
in a cold gated room
that engulfed
and mocked me
every chance it got
because i opened
my mouth
instead of
writing a poem.

this stigma.
this shame.
is stifling.

longing

melanin

i love your smile
and the metaphors
they rebuke and represent.
your sting is so sweet.
i am drunk off the honey
of your africanized being.
you are the manifestation
of the ancestors.

your skin is dark
as the velvet night.
your starred eyes
are tenants in constellations.
even the moon swells
whenever you're near.

all the makings of you
are love at first sight.
when i dream of you tonight,
i will hold you hostage
underneath my eyelids.

naked thoughts

i stand naked
before you.
i fear you may
see my heart.
i'm not well
with the secrets
my body tell.

the truth is
complicated.
it's easier to lie
and spread
my legs apart.

it is easier to push
your head lower
than to say
what's going on
inside my head.

it is easier to say
"fuck me harder"
than to say
"love me
and only me."

blood diamond

i yield to you
like you're the answer
to my savagery
because no one
explores my body
the way you do.

you dig so deep.
i don't know
what you're looking
for and i hope
you never find it.

i haven't found
myself yet and i know
it's in your bloodline
to colonize and exploit
untapped resources.

fellatio

as i dive for pearls
you place them
in my mouth
and hand me
a warm washcloth
for the ones
that escaped.

electric bodies

i can smell
what makes you a man
from across the room.
it boils my blood
to an electric blue
and engulfs my mouth
with desire.

plug yourself inside.
feel the electricity
traveling through
the circuit of our sexes.

summon the
ravenous beast
kneeling inside
aching to be freed
through the small
of my back.

arithmetic

you are the sum
of my lust.
subtracted
of reasoning.
divided by
my legs.
multiplied by
your thrusts.

you dilate
my third eye.
send shivers down
my inner thigh.
i smell you
in my dreams.
being more
than platonic
but erotic
human beings.

garden

i trembled
on the vine
waiting to be
sampled by you.
the fruit of my flesh
unpeeled in complete
surrender.

put your mouth on me
and break me open.
look into my eyes
and take me to paradise.

beautiful stranger

if i could fall in the abyss
i would capture your bliss
and grant you affection
i will no longer
ache for your lips
or lose my direction.

peel layers of me
i've never ever seen
turn me inside out
make the earth sprout
from underneath me.

i feel spellbound
when you surround
and rush through my veins
i want to lose myself
until nothing's the same
in ecstasy's name.

uncensored

i want to caress you
with the flesh
of my words
until you are found
naked
breathless
and too overwhelmed
to read the next line.

i want to push you
against the wall
of my words
pin you down
deprive you
of sight
and trace
each letter
across your lips.

thrust your eyes
against my pages
repeat with me
in unison
until you surrender
to love's doctrine.

transference

there's midnight
in his skin.
he even smells
like you.
an ache begins
to rise
in my bones.
i want to
close my eyes
and pretend
he's you
for a while.

longing

what should i do
with this longing?
tuck it away like a letter
that i'm too afraid to send?

hold it deep inside
another man's thrust
and pray i don't scream
out your name?

denounce it like a sin
and excommunicate
the heat rising
inside me?

you have not traveled
in my longing
and been stranded
on the corner of
unspoken words
and tell-tale stares.

you'll never collapse
under the weight of it
and remain suspended
in the air by a kiss
that will never
touch your lips.

residues

i am reminded
of your heat
when another man
touches me.
he brushes
off the embers
you once left behind.

hunger

your appetite
for me
is seasonal.
my longing
for you
is relentless.

meal

you remind me
of the salt fish stew
that my father made.
you tasted like home but
i resented the bones
you made me choke on.

when flour,
baking powder,
salt, and water
were pressed down by
the heels of strong palms
and fried in oil
that raged
like a revolution,
all was forgiven.
i devoured you.

metamorphic

dark cocoons
line my heart but
when i look at you,
butterflies flutter
and give birth
to spring.

beekeeper

put your mouth
on places
forbidden
to speak
to harvest
the honey
that only
drips for you.

inebriated

write my love letters
dripping with the blood
from your fermented heart.
i want to get drunk
off your words
and become undone
like ribbons
with each and
every syllable.

poetry

i compose my love
for you in stanzas
knowing where to
break us.

i lie in bed
with pen
and paper
because it never
puts on
its clothes
and leaves—

even when
i struggle
to write
the next line.

poetry ii

i can already
smell
and taste
the ways
you'll hurt me.

stay
away
from
me.

you have
all the makings
of my next muse.

love at first sight

the first time i saw you,
you siphoned the air
out of the room
and left me breathless.
i thought you were god.

for you

i would lasso the sun
and sell her rays
for profit
so you wouldn't
be blinded
by her anymore.

i would eat
all the stars
just for you to see
the light in my eyes.

i would bounce
my love off rainclouds
just to soften
your calcified heart.

what are you willing
to do for me?

the good guy

i am good at holding
onto nothing
like it's all i have
and running away
from something
like it's the plague.

i don't think
i deserve you
so i grasp at straws
instead of pressing
my lips against
the glass of your being
and slowly taking a sip.

i don't have
much to bring
but a broken heart
that feeds on flesh
and poetry.

i'll disappoint you
because it's all i know.

one wish

if you told me
right now
to come to you
i would drop
everything,
watch it shatter
like glass
and crawl
on the broken pieces
to show you
how much
love hurts.

entrails

i already know
how to set
your body on fire
and watch the trail
of ashes smolder but
i want to learn
how to find
a place in your heart.

path

i took the
scenic route
to your heart
and got lost
in your kiss.

elements

i search for water
in your mouth,
fire in your eyes,
earth on your body
and wind
when you whisper
in my ear.

smitten

i love losing myself
inside of you.
i am too smitten
by your landscape
to retrace my steps
or ask for directions.

i want to stay here
for a while
before reality
sets in.

tone deaf

we were
predestined
to align.
play and rewind.
asked to define
a love supreme,
malignant
or benign.

don't string
me along
but love me
like music.

my song
is as sweet
as hers
if you would
only listen.

but you sever
the chord
and chain
our melodies.

i believe
it is her song
that clouds
your ears.

nocturnal melody

i burn for you in the night—
unable to separate
the moon from the stars.

you have enchanted my night
despite rumors of your
infatuation with the sun.

my love for you
fondles the moon
and ejaculates in stars.
taste it.

constellations will dance
under our trance.
follow my lead.

your eclipsed heart
will wail for my stars
until you realize
you need
my cosmic grace.

chaos

charcoal

if the root
of all suffering
is attachment,
i see why
i'm drawn
to unavailable men.

unrequited love

unrequited love is like
kneeling on uncooked rice
and waiting for
the boiling water
of his kisses
to soften the pain
but he never comes.

he only peers
in the window
out of pity,
indifference,
or contempt
(it's hard to tell)
while you're trying
to crawl out of a poem
that he never wanted you
to write.

three's a crowd

you steal glimpses of her
and instantly feel inferior
in her presence. you study her
as if you'll be quizzed at a later
time.

her body takes up less space
than yours. you wonder if
yours should too. you wonder
if her melanin has more stories
than yours. if her eyes open
and shut the windows of his
soul. if her lips taste like milk
and honey.

if he looks into her eyes when
they make love or takes her
behind like he does you. if he
holds her closer than a secret
but never hides her behind
closed doors.

she looks around the room as
if she can smell your thoughts.
you hold your breath hoping it
would stop your heart from
beating so loudly for him.

you're his dirty little secret

hidden in the basement of his desire. you can't stop scratching at the door trying to evict her from the corridors of his heart.

your nails are bloody and your screams are useless. you have awakened a sleeping giant.

you've left him no other choice but to board up the door and egress window. you foolishly stay and collect dust until a nostalgic craving rises in his bones.

muse

i am not a woman
of many words
unless it is written.
you are a muse meant
to grace my pen.

words sprout
from my heart
and transport
to your pages
but you treat me
like i'm corrosive.

i have a solution.
bind me
acid-free.
maybe in time
you'll see
the splendor
of my words.

misogynoirist

"black women
are only good
for sex."

his words
cut into my flesh
removed my entrails
and stripped the
yellow, red, and blue
of my being.

i felt invisible.
unlovable.
a petal punctured
by the thorn on his side
even though
we bloomed from
the same concrete.

i thought our hues
were created to fuse
into one another,
brotha.

daddy complex

when the crackle
in your voice
grows loud
with lightning
and thunder,
i stand at attention
and hold my breath.
you sound like my father.
i don't know whether
to curse you
or run to my room.

hypothetical

dear painter,
i am the paint
that aches to drip
for your brush.

will your soft strokes
on the flesh
of my canvas
leave me bleeding
after you wash
me away?

dear writer,
i hold onto
every word
pressed against
your pages.

if ink dripped
from your fingertips
and i rendered
my body as paper,
would you write
a poem for me?

secret lovers

you treat me as if
you barely know
the scent
of my skin,
the scorch
of my lips
and the grind
of my hips
wantonly
responding
to you.

you treat me as if
i barely know
the definition
of your hands,
the silk onyx
of your skin
and the way
you crash
into me
conjuring
the longing
seething underneath
our skin.

stargazer

she's a starry night sky.
you admire her magic
as you thread over me—
never rubbing my earth
between your fingers.

next time tell her
to come down
from unspooling stars
from the moon
to deal with
your bullshit.

buried

you bury your rod
inside of me
instead of your heart
as if i'm a graveyard
to bury your pleasure.

i absorb the salt
from your veins
when life becomes
too heavy of a pillar
to carry.

i am the sentence
dripping in honey
that you want
every drop of.

know this—
that you hide more
than your bones
when you're inside of me.

certain men

(i.)

there are men
who will come to you
late in the night
to hide you
from the light of day
as if you are a vampire
but they're the one
holding you down,
biting your neck
and sucking
all they can
from of your veins
until you're lifeless
from loving them.

(ii.)

there are men
who can smell
your insecurity
lynching
every fiber
of your being.
they'll devour you
and claim
you're the sweetest
yet strangest fruit

they have ever tasted
but they'll never
untie you
because once you
hit the ground,
you'll realize
you deserve more.

(iii.)

there are men
who will come alive
when they're inside of you
but say you're dead to them
when you step outside
their boundaries.
you'll have to learn
how to balance yourself
on eggshells
before you end up
with egg on your face.

if you ever meet them,
run until your feet
are blistered.
never let them clench
you with their teeth.

combustible

if fire and gunpowder
do not sleep together,
then why are you
between my legs?

you know i'll always burn
a bright blue for you
and you'll always
have ammunition
on the tip of your tongue.

hypocrite

i said i would
leave you alone
and pack what's left
of my heart
and move on.

i said i would
let you be
but conjure
you up
in my dreams.

but on these pages,
you'll always breathe
even though
unrequited love
is suffocating me.

tilted

my love is messy.
it smears everything
in sight and leaves a stench.

my love is clumsy.
it bumps into everything
and apologizes excessively.

i've yet to find
the equilibrium.
i don't know
how to confine
my love.

brokenhearted

once a heart learns
how to break,
it does not know
how to forget.
it endures
sleepless nights,
memorizes
every morsel
of despair
and relives
every moment
in the stillness
of tears.

last kiss

i am lost
in translation
of our
last kiss.
my lips
have not been
the same
to decipher this.

i've learned
to kiss you
with my eyes.
there are times
you do not see me
as i kiss you
with a quiet desperation
that you would
never understand.

side effect

there's a void
in your eyes
and it hurts
to swim in them.

there is no
reciprocity.
only a lingering
hope and dream
of your love
enveloping me.

tears swell
in the wells
of my eyes.
love is a
constant
side effect
of mine.

resentment

i took an excursion
on your skin,
spun you around
and molded a
continent of you
but these days
i'm tempted to
push you
over the edge
and watch
you shatter
the same way
you did me.

shameless

you,
the starving artist
resented
my hunger pains
but continued
to feed on me.

i,
the unrequited lover
camouflaged
myself in lust
before love
unveiled me.

when you met laura

you shook the tree
of my longing
and caught every leaf.
when winter came,
you no longer sat
underneath me.

the earth tones
clinging to the flesh
of my bones
couldn't compete
with the beauty
and geometry
of a snowflake.

nothing

i chiseled away
parts of myself
trying to be
everything to you
until it could no longer
be rendered as art.

when we fell apart
at the seams,
you howled at me
like i was the moon
and said that i
was nothing to you.

pangea

you ruptured
the love lakes
of my longing
and scattered
the continents
of my heart.

you told me not to
fall in love with you
but you knew
the contours
of my heart.

smoke

they say that
patience is a virtue
but they never tell you
that the heat of
waiting will burn you
if you linger too long.

sinking

our foundation is rocky
because we made a home
in each other's skin.
the damage is beginning
to show.

the cracks in your walls
are more prominent
than your smile
and my heart
has buckled
under the weight
of my tears.

i've closed
other doors
in an attempt
to be yours
but you're always
eyeing the window
and i can't cure
your wanderlust.

paralyzer

i have stars
in my eyes
for a guy
who rather
suffocate
and dim them
because they
burned
too bright
with love.

he fossilizes
my hopes
underneath
his skin
to keep from
unearthing
my heart.

scavenger

i rummaged
for pieces of you
and made leaves of grass
that turned into trees
that lynched me
by my heartstrings.

i hid in the shadows
until you summoned my light.
i put out fires you spewed
and cooled you down
with my tongue.

i made excuses for you.
i accepted apologies
you've never uttered
and smeared
the writing on the wall
before everyone woke up.

gentrified

you want to look
into my eyes
when we make love
but i am afraid
that you'll see
that i'm the
haunted house
at the end of the street
that no one
wants to visit
unless it's halloween.

the forest green
of your eyes
is now the grass.
your skin is the
white picket fence.
your smile is the garden.
you have stripped
my interior
and exterior
and painted them
with your kisses.

i don't know
who i am anymore.
you smell
like gentrification.

barrier

i watch you sleep
and long to hold you
but fear barricades me.
i peacefully retreat,
hold my tears hostage
and force them
to drown
the deep and
shallow parts
of my heart.

tunnel vision

this love is deferred.
my visions of love
are astigmatic
and blurred
but yet and still,
i can't take my eyes
off you.

invasion

you've invaded
my solitude
and veins.

the rhythm
of my heart
has not been
the same.

in all my reveries
i tune my breath
to suit your melody

when words
become obsolete,
i will follow
the echoes
of your heartbeat.

in another life

you say
you crave me
but deprive
yourself of me.

your hunger
mesmerizes me.

hold my hair
as i regurgitate
our past lives
because the way
you breathe on me
feels too familiar.

alchemy

i knew his heart
was yours
but i wanted
to become
an alchemist
to make gold
of the pieces
i received
because
all i ever felt
was the dark side
of his leaded heart.

emissions

sometimes i choke
on the smoke
of our unfiltered
moments.
passion confers
as i breathe you in
but you waste me
like carbon
as i emit my love
to the purple haze
of yesteryear.

what i miss

i miss the way
you ripened the fruit
of my inhibitions
and pressed them
into wine.

i miss searching for
my mother tongue
in each and every kiss.

i miss your fingernails
tracing the veins
of my scattered lineage.

germination

my bruised ego
trips and bears
the fruit of regret.

i am ashamed
to claim the seed
that refused to grow

so i swallow
my feelings whole
on an empty stomach
and expel them
onto blank pages.

epiphany

gun & broom

you jumped
the broom
after you swept
me away like trash.

her grass seemed
greener until
a drought came
and cracked the earth
beneath you.

her eyes burned
brighter until they
ran out of fuel
and left you stranded.

you jumped
the gun
but i dodged
a bullet.

rumor has it
her new husband
is tending
to her yard now.

i am mine

the other day
i saw someone
who reminded
me of you.
time and
my breath
stood still.

as he took
a slow drag
on a cigarette,
i wished
it was my lips
burning at the end
and filling his lungs.
i wanted to be
his craving
and cancer.

in the beginning,
all i wanted was
to be yours.
it took time to realize
that i have to stop
giving myself away
as if i didn't belong
to myself.

rose quartz

i often wander
into my heart
and gaze through
rose-colored
spectrums.

i often wonder
if your heart
have enough hues
to be human.

don't move.

we can take turns
healing each other.

your belly
is too full
of my love
and i'm always
starving for yours.

self-sabotage

healing requires
every cell
in your body
but i'm so used
to dealing
with myself
in fragments.

sometimes i lift
the scab to revisit
the pink flesh of pain
to feel more alive.

would i know
what peace looked like
if it gently knocked
on my heart?

would i open
the door
or pretend
i wasn't home?

true colors

i am beyond the pale.
my kinky hair,
broad nose
and full lips
are remnants
of my ancestors.

my pride swells
like yeast
in the heat
of your prejudice.

when i found out my hue
prevented you
from choosing me,
it made me finally see
your true colors.

lost

i was so preoccupied
with loving you
that i failed
to love myself.

your eyes
became my sight.
your mouth
became my breath.
your body became
my sanctuary.

when it was over
i didn't know
who i was anymore.

i was left blind,
breathless and
aimlessly wandering.

to be honest,
i didn't know
who i was before
but i must
do the work
to find out.

soft

i have to find ways
to be soft
without
using my body.

without
wearing my heart
on my sleeve
for wolves to feed on.

without
hardening parts
of me that screams
for it the most.

when you're feeling low

your mental health
is as delicate
as porcelain.
it only takes
one misstep
for it to shatter
and render you
motionless.
into shards
of nothingness.

there are days
you'll wish
to un-breathe
every breath,
unopen your eyes
and fade into black.

i beg of you
to keep filling
your air with lungs.
line the darkness
with stars until
the sun rises again.
your heart of gold
will repair
the broken pieces.

published

i abandoned my words
because you did not like
the sound of them.
to you they were
a blasphemous prayer
that i wailed for on
bloodied bended knees.

so i buried them deep
but this book
of ache and longing
collapsed from its spine
and found you and me
hiding underneath
the weight of the words.

it's time to set
these pages free
and i don't give a damn
how you feel about it.

waves

you navigate
the waves
of my emotions.

i try not to linger
but my fingers
ache to touch you.

i'll lie on my side
and wait for your tide
to rush through.

i knew the cause
and effect
of my makeshift beliefs.

i was bound
to drown but
the warrior in me
prevailed.

the burial

you said
i was dead
to you
and buried me
and every memory.

i scurried
to the surface
and offered truth
as reprieve
but you shuffled
more dirt on me.

i never felt
more alive
and dead
at the same time.

refugee

where should i go?
your skin is the only
place i know.
it's a shallow grave
i'll never stop
bringing flowers to.
it's in my bloodline
to honor the dead.

lesson learned

it is a proven theorem.
the sums of our parts
were negative
but i was willing
to learn the pieces
to make us whole.

the science of us
was complicated.
i formulated
every hypothesis,
grasped
and strangled
every hope
and endured
love's asphyxiation.

i've learned
to breathe
without you.
exit my wounds
so i can heal.

search party

love ridden
i searched for you
in corridors,
open doors
and in endless seas
of similes
and metaphors
but we never were
on the same page.

colonista

i forged
states of felicity
and found colonies
in our nothingness.

i declared my body
as the flag,
the swirl
of our tongues
as the language
and our love sounds
as the national anthem.

but you rebelled.
you tore into
my heartland
and pledged allegiances
to other territories.

i had to abdicate
my love for you
so i could start
loving myself.

the chaos of longing

this voyage—
the chaos
of longing
is no longer
anchored at sea.

i've sailed
the desolate shore
of your heart
and got swept away
by your arctic current.

i floated to the surface
with my heart's
message in a bottle.

ordered

there is chaos
in our bones.
grind them
into ashes.
cry over them
until they're dissolved.

if you're all cried out,
find the nearest
body of water
that swells in salt.

repeat until
the chaos
comes into order.
heal.

self-love

if you eat men
and still feel
like you're starving,
you're craving something
that they cannot give.

don't expect men
to fill vessels
that were gifted
to you to overflow.

darling,
find passion
and self-worth within
instead of
locking them
inside of men
who like swallowing keys
so they can keep you
all to themselves.

elements ii

there's a universe
swirling inside you.

you have to learn to be
your own earth,
wind, fire
and water.

you are a natural
phenomenon—
not a natural disaster.

glutton

you can't stuff yourself
alive with lust
to fill the empty spaces.

if you love yourself first,
your heart will always be
at full capacity—

not a blinking vacancy sign
that reeks of loneliness,
filth and despair.

stillness

don't stay
in a moment
for too long.
you tend
to lose yourself.
darling,
you must
be tired
of feeling
your way out
of the dark
long after
they've left.

devotee

you can't make
anyone love you
no matter how
many times
and ways
you lay down
your body,
your heart
and your world
at their feet.

they will only
step over you
until they're ready
for you to wash
their feet with your hair
and to set them on fire
with your tongue.

they can tell
by the look
in your eyes,
the way you
surrender
when you part
your thighs
and by the poems
that you write
that you deify them.

truth

when you find
your voice,
keep it.
hold it close like
your very first
teddy bear.

swell with pride
with each letter
pressed against pages
that broke
the levees
in your throat.

don't shrink
your truth
to make it fit
nice and neatly
in others
as if it's origami.

unfold and
free yourself.

self-love ii

self-love is a journey.
sometimes you have to take it
in the heat of the day.
you will find yourself
on the side of the road
thirsty, sweaty
and out of breath.

you will crave
instant gratification.
you will want to slither
your way back to your choice
of poison, throw your head
back and take a desperate gulp
because their skin is all you
know.

please don't.
it's time to learn new things.

it's time to give the love
you denied yourself
but frantically searched
for in others.
it's time to realize that
love was never trapped
underneath their
lips and fingertips.
you held it hostage
the entire time.

the galaxy is yours

star your own sky.
drink the shooting stars.
lasso the moon.
take a bite.
feel the juice
of self-love
running
down your chin
and laugh madly.

you're still alive.
you're still alive.
you're still alive.

Made in the USA
San Bernardino, CA
14 May 2017